Improve
Attention to Detail

Improve Attention to Detail

A straightforward system to develop attention to detail in yourself, employees, and across an organization.

Chris Denny

Improve Attention to Detail: A straightforward system to develop attention to detail in yourself, employees, and across an organization

ISBN: 978-0-9905260-4-9

William & Louis Publishing

Love and thanks to my Darling, Ela. Every moment.

And, a special thanks to all of you who contributed your ideas, experiences, encouragement, time, *and attention*.

Table of Contents

Introduction

One day I was working through some challenges with an employee whose lack of attention to detail at the time was appallingly low. While he was *technically capable,* the work he turned in was essentially worthless without heavy revisions and he didn't even pay enough attention to the requested corrections to get them right on the second, and often third, attempts. I don't like to give up on people -- and he was an otherwise talented and technically strong employee -- so I searched (and searched and searched) for training on how to improve attention to detail. When I couldn't find relevant training, I made several attempts at getting him to "pay more attention" and "make fewer mistakes" but just couldn't figure it out. Eventually we had to part ways, and I was disappointed about that because he had loads of potential, if not for his unacceptable errors. I like to think he is highly successful now.

I was convinced there was a way to help people like him improve their attention to detail, to be better at what they do, make more money, advance their careers, and get more fulfillment from a job well done. After all, I used to NOT be a detail-oriented person, so what made me become detail-oriented? I thought about my own growth and then started interviewing people, taking surveys, reading books that seemed related, and listening to audiobooks -- thousands of hours of work and research -- on the topics of focus, awareness, attention, productivity, error reduction, psychology, training, organizational psychology, and more. Even with the system and framework I've developed, I'm still looking for ways to improve it. Every project, every client, every person I talk to, is an opportunity to learn more and make the system better to help more people. In fact, as I bring this book to a close, there are concepts and discussion points I'm considering adding, but some will have to wait until the next book or edition.

The fantastic thing is that it's clear that *you can improve attention to detail* in individuals and groups, and the Attention To Detail Training and materials I've developed provide a simple system for you to get started. I'm exceptionally proud of the system, which I've been delivering through corporate workshops, speaking engagements, coaching, and online courses since 2017. The Attention To Detail Training system and framework was designed with the goals of helping individuals and organizations become more detail-oriented to decrease errors, increase productivity, and improve the overall quality of products, services, and experiences delivered.

Purpose

First, I want this book to be simple and fairly non-technical so that anyone, regardless of your education level, technical level, or profession can use this book to help improve your own attention to detail or that of your employees. By its nature, some of the material is somewhat technical, but I've tried to tone the language down so you won't feel like you need a few classes in psychology or quality control to keep up.

The purpose of this book -- and my videos, coaching, online training, and workshops -- is to help individuals and organizations to be more productive and more successful overall by becoming more detail-oriented. For some, that means reducing errors or improving task accuracy, while for others it means increasing the total quality of the services, experiences, or products they offer.

By its nature, the impact of attention to detail improvements starts at the individual level. The work I do can impact an entire organization, but it does so largely by improving or enhancing the task-level accuracy and effectiveness of individual performers.

It is amazingly rewarding. I love that I'm able to help an organization by helping individuals. It is wonderful to help an organization be more successful -- whether that means it produces better products and provides better service for its customers, is better able to retain and hire more people, or improves profitability through bottom- and/or top-line improvements. By far, though, the largest reward for me -- what motivates and compels me -- is the ability to help *individuals* do better, perform better, succeed in their immediate task goals, and maybe even make more money. Heck, there are some people who have taken my courses simply so they can improve their performance enough *to keep a job* they like. That is just as rewarding as helping people who simply want to make more money because I've helped them fulfill their basic needs, perhaps even contributed in a tiny way to helping them take care of their families.

The *first* time someone told me *I had changed her life* I knew I had found my purpose. Simple as that. Whether you are striving for personal improvement or want to positively adjust the culture of an entire organization, this book is an extension of that purpose -- to help you do better and *be better* at whatever it is you do.

The Costs of
Poor Attention to Detail

96% of executives and 97% of people managers say being more detail-oriented will make you more successful in your career.[1]

The errors and omissions made because of lack of attention to detail can have any number of negative impacts on a company's bottom and/or top lines. Common costs and losses due to preventable errors and omissions related to poor attention to detail include:

- Lost customers
- Harm to reputation or brand
- Missed sales opportunities
- Leaving "money on the table" during a sale
- Wasted management or employee time
- Decreased employee morale
- Rebuilds, re-works, or re-prints
- Freight & delivery costs
- Non-compliance
- Legal risks or lawsuits
- Injuries (or death)
- Missed opportunities for improvement or innovation

---

[1] *Survey #19*. DetailOriented.org. Collected as of December 17, 2018.

The items on the list are in logical groups based on the source(s) of the costs -- Sales & Reputation, Management & Employees, Production & Operational Costs, and Legal & Safety.

The costs within each group are similar or related and could be broken down further, especially if you delve into specific industries. Below is an expanded discussion of the various costs, organized by group.

For the sake of discussion and analysis the costs are separate here but, in real life, mistakes generally have multiple costs. For instance, you will likely surmise that many of costs bring additional labor costs. The nature of the additional labor varies widely and can be stifling to a company's bottom line. Whether the additional labor costs are spent to rebuild products, handle returns, correct forms, or deal with lawsuits, they are an inefficient use of limited resources and should be minimized or eliminated altogether. Defective products that reach the market will create the obvious replacement costs -- materials, production and delivery labor, fuel, etc. -- and are likely to create harder-to-measure costs such as loss of reputation and possibly even regulatory or legal concerns.

Sales & Reputation Related Costs

This set of costs is primarily related to sales effectiveness, capturing opportunities, and customer service and how a company's ability (or inability) to do them well can impact top-line results. A few questions to consider while reading are:

- What is the lifetime value (LTV) of a customer in your business?
- What is the value of your brand and how much value do you lose when people start sharing bad experiences (in person or online)?
- What common mistakes or omissions do you make that result in lost customers?
- What activities do you engage in (or not engage in) that are inconsistent with your brand?
- Do you know the areas in which you should innovate?
- What kinds of information or details should your salespeople collect from customers?

Lost customers: Customers leave -- and take their money with them -- when they experience too many mistakes, omissions (conscious or unconscious), or situations that leave them frustrated, inconvenienced, or otherwise feeling shortchanged in their transaction with a company. The source(s) of their poor experience may be marketing, sales, operations, billing, or any other part of the company and total experience. Customers can also be "lost" in the future sense when they hear about the bad experiences of others and decide to take their business elsewhere.

Harm to reputation or brand: Each dissatisfied customer has all the information needed to leave a bad review or tell a friend about the bad experience. The cumulative effect of bad reviews, press, or even word of a mouth can be devastating to a company's reputation and sales, especially if the negative message is related to the company's core brand messaging or products (i.e., what they are best at or best known for).

Missed sales opportunities: At the individual transaction level, salespeople, customer service representatives, and other customer-facing staff often miss sales opportunities because they do not fully understand (or listen to) the prospective customer's inquiry, OR because they do not ask qualifying questions that might reveal the true nature of the question -- and thereby create the opportunity for a sale and a happy customer.

In terms of the three types of attention to detail, which we will cover later, the employee often sees the customer's initial question as a contrastive issue with a "yes" or "no" answer. However, the question is usually an analytical issue for which the customer needs a solution. This is related to the old adage most professional salespeople (especially "old school" salespeople) are likely familiar with: "When the customer asks for a drill bit, what he really wants is a *hole*."

You might also say you're missing sales and growth opportunities when you fail to see opportunities to innovate your products or services. Often, a company's highest margin products and services come from recognizing that their customers want something they may not even realize themselves. Or, perhaps the customer asks for something no one makes. Instead of saying, "we don't have that" or "there's no such thing" take some time to consider whether you can deliver that service or product and if there are other customers who would want to buy it. Doing this effectively requires a culture in which the "frontline" people are listening and thinking carefully about what customers are asking for, and where other departments and leadership are open to considering the information and ideas brought to them.

Leaving "money on the table" during a sale: An engaged salesperson goes beyond the initially requested product or service to find the full scope of the customer's need or project. The essence of this is brilliantly systematized for franchise and other frontline workers through simple and familiar upsell lines such as, "Would you like fries with that?" In complex or technical sales, the professional, engaged, interested salesperson will discover -- in one way or another -- the entire scope of a project. The "upsell" is in the discovery of the larger opportunity within the inquiry -- perhaps the full project scope, the *real* pain points, the main decision maker, and so on -- and the subsequent development of a solution or total package offering. In contracts the devil may be in the details but in sales the details are often where the money is.

Additionally, this aspect of attention to detail can, and should, be applied to your systems and marketing assets. For instance, after delving into the metrics of your website or point of sale system, you may spot trends and/or tendencies that indicate your customers' pain points, solutions needs, and what products they tend to buy together.

Management & Employee Costs (Labor Costs)

The two costs included in this set are primarily related to the effective or ineffective utilization of management and employees' time when mistakes are made by an individual or group -- especially when they are made regularly. For the sake of simplicity, I focus here on time and/or labor costs related to internal administrative and processing errors (usually paperwork and reporting errors), and leave materials and production costs for the next section.

The costs associated with time and labor are difficult to track in many cases. The tangible, day-to-day impacts are primarily made apparent through lack of execution (i.e. things do not get done in a timely manner) and the palpable frustrations of everyone involved. Consider these questions while reading:

- What are the most common mistakes you see in your organization?
- What procedures or tasks in your organization tend to induce mistakes or require re-do's?
- Are the common mistakes usually made by the same person(s) or does everyone make them?

- How much time do you, your employees, and/or management spend correcting others' mistakes?
- Can you assign a dollar value to the mistakes and corrections?
- Would additional training or the application of a system correct or reduce the mistakes?

Wasted management or employee time: Corrections, edits, re-do's, improvements, or even apologies have to be identified and/or made by *someone* -- whether a coworker, manager, or the employee who made the mistake.

In addition to the time required to identify and address mistakes directly, there is often additional time spent on double-checks once a pattern of mistakes has been established and trust in an individual (or group) has been lost. In other words, it takes time for someone to look over an employee's shoulder.

Decreased employee morale: Based on surveys I've been running since 2011, decreased employee morale is one of the most commonly cited costs of low attention to detail.

Employees generally like to be productive, to "do a good job", and work around others who do the same. An individual's productivity and quality of work can be a source of pride, or at least a contributor to his or her own feeling of self-worth and self-efficacy. So, when employees are repeatedly tasked (either by management or their own internal drive) with correcting the mistakes of a coworker *who is expected to be competent,* they may become frustrated with the individual *as well as* the situation. Correcting others' mistakes takes away from their own productivity and workflow and maybe, occasionally, even from their own private time. When simple training is adequate to remedy the situation, coworkers will generally handle the situation without fuss by informally training the offender on the correct way to complete the task. But wouldn't it be better if the training was effectively covered in new employee orientation or an employee manual so the problem never came up?

The range of outcomes varies widely, but if mistakes are allowed to continue, expect them to negatively impact employee job satisfaction, retention rate, perceptions of management, culture, and/or overall productivity. They should be addressed quickly and appropriately. Some issues may be short-term and directly related to a stressful life event such as divorce or a death in the family. Others may be more complex and require more intense scrutiny with time spent on developing a solution.

It is worth making a special comment about new employees because a lower level of competence is generally expected of them -- *until it's not*. "New" does not always mean young, of course, so we may be referring to a seasoned expert in a given field. She may be the most competent person in the *industry* regarding her field of expertise, but struggles a bit with the software system her new employer uses for project planning. New employees are generally granted a certain amount of leniency with their mistakes because they are learning -- new systems, processes, rules, technical information and jargon, equipment, culture, and maybe even specific preferences (or quirks) of management or customers. While teaching a new employee is distracting -- and maybe even frustrating -- everyone understands and excuses mistakes almost completely *for a while -- until that employee is expected to be competent*. For every position there is a point at which the new person isn't "new" anymore and their mistakes are on them.

Production & Operational Costs

These costs are directly related to service deliverables (e.g., prepared tax documents or legal contracts), materials, fuel, or other assets involved in the production of physical goods. The obvious additional labor costs are discussed in the previous section and I'll leave them there. While reading, consider these questions:

- Are there specific products or product lines in which production errors are made more commonly than others?
- Do you have a way to track the error rate? (errors as percentage of products or jobs completed as well as metrics about the nature of the errors)
- Have employees been properly trained on your products, operations, and QC processes?
- If you have identified the cause of error(s), are you sure you are correct?

- What improvements can be made to production, design, delivery, logistics, quality control, or other operational processes?
- Can training or the application of a system significantly reduce or cure the issue?

Rebuilds, re-works, or re-prints: When mistakes are made in the production of service deliverables or physical products, there are direct and measurable material and/or labor costs involved. The earlier the mistake is caught, the more costs can be minimized. Ideally, the mistake is caught before the product moves to its next phase of production, and certainly before it is delivered to the end user or customer, which can negatively impact reputation and/or future sales in addition to the direct costs associated with correcting the mistake.

The range of possible errors is vast. An employee at a production plant may assemble a few parts with the wrong washer and have to correct that after it is caught by some quality control measure. A local deck builder may misinterpret (or mis-remember) the plans and build part of the customer's deck with the wrong design. A bookkeeper may have left significant income from an LLC or other asset out of the delivered documents. The marketing department might print and mail an invitation to all of the company's customers with the wrong event date. A large manufacturer of car parts might make a design and/or production error that leads to a recall affecting millions of car owners.

Some mistakes are simple for an individual or organization to avoid completely, while avoiding others may require significant analysis as well as trial and error. How avoidable mistakes are depends largely upon the complexity of the product or deliverable and the knowledge and experience we have around it. In other words, do we know all the possible things that can go wrong? If so, we can largely avoid them. If not, *and we want to avoid them all* – perhaps success is highly critical – then we need to apply additional analysis and perhaps bring on board the knowledge and experience of experts and/or consultants who can help identify and address all the possible situations and challenges.

Freight & delivery costs: Additional freight and delivery costs may result from poor product quality (returns and re-delivery), damage during transit, miscommunication between buyer and salespeople, inaccurate product descriptions, incorrect delivery date or addresses, poor inventory management (e.g., order delivered in two shipments instead of just one), wrong parts pulled from stock, incomplete or inaccurate bill of lading or customs forms, customer preference, and many more scenarios.

Unfortunately, freight and delivery employees probably cannot affect the quality of the products delivered (other than through feedback) but they can ensure that systems are in place to pull the right part(s), double-check delivery addresses and dates, verify details of paperwork, inform the customer of delivery time, and more.

The possible causes of additional freight costs are numerous, but, in general, mistakes made from the point of pulling parts for an order through delivery to the end user are almost completely avoidable through rules, systems, training, and an aware staff.

Legal & Safety Costs and Risks

Attention to detail is exceptionally important when dealing with many safety and/or regulatory requirements to ensure the safe and uninterrupted or, at least, un-fined operation of an organization. The risk of fines, suspension of operations, and litigation is real, and extra effort and attention to detail can help maintain an organization's compliance, reduce risks, and keep safety-related events and concerns to a minimum.

Questions to consider while reading this section include:

- Is your organization aware of all the official regulatory and compliance requirements for the business and industry? Are you compliant?
- Which of your organization's operational activities or which services or products present the potential for legal risks or lawsuits?
- Are there any known safety concerns? Do you know the latest safety regulations?
- What steps can be taken to help ensure compliance and/or increase awareness of compliance requirements?

Non-compliance: Regulations and license requirements abound in industries from plumbing to medicine to law to nearly any kind of manufacturing or energy-related operations. In fact, nearly every company in the United States -- and nearly every other country -- is regulated to some degree from the moment they open their doors for business. For instance, a company is immediately responsible for the recording, documenting, and filing requirements of the city, county, state, and country. Requirements may include official business name registration, possibly a business entity formation, and registration with a state and/or federal tax entity (or all). Failure to properly comply with regulatory and compliance requirements or laws may result in fines, penalties, lawsuits, or even suspension from continuing business operations.

Common compliance concerns for businesses include:

- Health & safety
- Data security & privacy
- Tax and accounting requirements
- Environmental
- Legal
- Industry regulation and/or certification
- Contractual

Compliance is not just about whether or not you registered or have the proper licenses. You may need to post a notice for all employees to see, your license number may be required on your marketing materials and invoices, or yearly training may be required. Make sure the compliance requirements for everything you do are known, understood, and managed appropriately.

Legal risks or lawsuits: Legal risks are everywhere and in many different forms. Negligence and discrimination are two of the most common reasons companies are sued.[2] In many cases, the company was unaware of their own negligence or discrimination due to simple human error, ineffectual systems, or inadequate knowledge or training.

An attorney friend told me a common mistake she sees attorneys make is that a long and valuable contract might refer to details in an attached addendum but then forget to include that addendum. When a dispute happens in the future, the cited addendum is nowhere to be found and there is understandable disagreement over what is found or provided after the fact. This turns into additional legal costs and, potentially, a bad relationship between the involved parties.

As another example, a small business owner delegated the hiring of a new employee to the recently-promoted department manager. Being experienced in the job function and knowing all the requirements of the role himself, he was assumed to be fully capable of hiring an adequate

---

[2] "5 Most Common Lawsuits". www.thebalancesmb.com, https://www.thebalancesmb.com/five-most-common-lawsuits-3886658. Accessed 1/11/2019.

employee. However, he was unaware of discrimination laws and the related protected classes. During the casual conversation part of an interview with a young woman, he mentioned his kids and asked her if she and her new husband intended to have children. When she did not get the job (there was a more qualified candidate) she filed a legal claim against the company stating she was discriminated against because she is a woman and because she said she was planning to get pregnant (gender and pregnancy are both protected classes). The business owner was reasonably familiar with the rules of what you can and cannot ask -- or, at least, knows to stay away from personal questions -- but did not think to mention the issue to the new department manager. An hour or two of training on basic employment and hiring practices likely would have avoided this issue altogether.

Having policies, systems, training, and knowledgeable people in place (perhaps through outside counsel) helps companies avoid legal issues.

Injury or death: The injury or death of a person or persons is a large enough cost alone, but it may also bring about legal expenses, a large monetary judgment, increased insurance costs, and possibly even harm to a company's reputation.

Industries with high levels of risk or rates of injury or death tend to become regulated quickly -- think air travel, freight, oil production, nuclear energy, and so on -- but there is still plenty of room for human error, negligence, or lack or training or knowledge to create unsafe workplaces and accidents in any business setting.

Impact on the Individual

At the personal level, employees who lack attention to detail, regardless of the reason, may be:

- Generally unsuccessful in their work
- Unhappy or unfulfilled
- Frustrated
- Fired or demoted
- Injured
- Aggravating and demoralizing for other employees
- Poorly paid (and maybe rightly so)
- Passed over for promotions

78% of executives and 80% of managers believe that lack of attention to detail is costing their organization money.[3] Managers, directors, business owners, and employees all say they typically prefer to hire and work with detail-oriented people because those are the best employees -- the ones who catch mistakes, save time, and do work right the first time. Not only do they themselves require less management time, but they reduce the time required by management to deal with problems throughout the company or department. They are also easier for employees

---

[3] *Survey #19*. DetailOriented.org. Collected as of December 17, 2018.

to work with because they tend to pull their own weight and keep things moving along which helps goals get met and allows everyone to go home on time.

There is undeniable value in employees who are detail-oriented. Since most people are not naturally or strongly detail-oriented, it is important to provide development and create systems that make up the difference and, in the end, create an organization -- a team -- that is detail-oriented. Through the use of systems, consistent communication, and a focus on getting the little things right, companies can create a detail-oriented culture where things run more smoothly and people are more likely to be successful.

Common Excuses for Mistakes Related to Attention to Detail

Sadly, repeated workplace mistakes or inaccuracies commonly get chalked up to one of these ambiguous excuses or labels:

- Stupidity
- Apathy
- Laziness
- Negligence (a scary one)
- Unclear instructions or misunderstanding
- Lack of necessary information
- Tiredness or substance issues
- Stress
- Some mix of the above

No one wants one of these labels applied to them. Most employees are capable and smart individuals, but there's always room for improvement. Unfortunately, individuals or even groups get labeled with one or more of these because of repeated mistakes or generally low productivity.

As you'll see, the application and/or improvement of one or more of the five fundamentals of attention to detail may be all that is needed to correct or resolve the issue (and remove the negative labels).

You Can Become
More Detail-Oriented

"Errors arise from informational problems either in the mind of the individual or in the world at large." -- James Reason[4]

Attention to Detail is Not Perfection

I'd like to clarify that attention to detail or being detail-oriented is not about being or becoming a perfectionist. The idea of perfection is unrealistic. It is unattainable and even demotivating. It can be paralyzing.

You can't be perfect. You can't create something that is perfect. If something is perfect, there is no room for improvement -- and *there is always room for improvement*.

Furthermore, I believe many people label themselves as a "perfectionist" as if it's some sort of honorary badge they can use as an excuse for not getting things done in a timely manner. They procrastinate and hem and haw over some task or project and when asked why it's not complete yet they defend themselves with the paper-thin shield of "I'm a perfectionist." Likewise, others use it as the reason for their unnecessary anxiety. They procrastinate on a project and

---

[4] Reason, James. A Life in Error: From Little Slips to Big Disasters. Ashgate, 2013.

then flash their badge of perfectionism saying they're so stressed about making it perfect they just can't seem to get started.

Attention to detail is about improvement -- whether the improvement comes through reducing errors in a task or system or improving the quality of a service, product, or experience. It is about doing better, making something better, or being better.

You should consider striking the word "perfect" from your vocabulary. It sounds lovely when you want to highlight how great something is, but, as a goal, it is unrealistic.

So, what is a better word? One that fits? One that is realistic and attainable?

How about excellence? Excellence.

Excellence is the goal of attention to detail. Excellence means being outstanding or exceptionally good. It is about being great *or even better than great*.

You can put forth an excellent effort and do it again tomorrow and the next day and the day after, constantly improving whatever you are working on. Excellence can be focused, and with the right focus, effort, and determination you can achieve excellence in your work, in systems, in the achievement of your goals, in productivity, in your company. Excellence is attainable -- by you, in fact.

3 Types of Attention to Detail

"You don't have to be a genius or a visionary or even a college graduate to be successful. You just need a framework and a dream." -- Michael Dell

I believe the lack of identifying and separating the three types of attention to detail has contributed to the frustration people feel when they are trying to improve their own attention to detail -- and even more so when they are trying to develop attention to detail in others.

When asking or instructing employees to be more detail-oriented managers usually just say something similar to, "You have to pay more attention to detail." But, what does that mean? Within the context of the mistake or series of events that initiated the instruction (or plea), it sounds straightforward. What the manager typically means is something more specific such as, "Look more closely for spelling errors in your emails," "Verify numbers before putting them into reports," "Double-check every item on quotes before sending them," or more generally, "Listen more closely to what [customer/manager/attorney] says during meetings."

There are three types of attention to detail. Most people and/or professions primarily use only one or two, while some use all three regularly.

When dealing with specific challenges or situations, understanding and labeling which type of attention to detail would apply can help you remain focused, reduce errors and/or wasted time, and improve the quality of your outcome or solution. The three types of attention to detail are:

- Contrastive
- Analytical
- Additive

The three types of attention to detail build upon one another in one direction. Contrastive is needed for analytical, and contrastive and analytical are needed for additive. The reason for this will become clear as you study these and consider their applications. And remember: You want to move toward contrastive.

Contrastive Attention to Detail

Contrastive attention to detail is necessary for tasks and situations in which there is a comparison (a check or verification), a clear "right or wrong" answer, or for identifying unique elements. It is objective. 2+2 is always 4, the numbers either match or they don't, the specifications are either met or not, the address is either right or wrong, the accounts balance or they don't, it's red or it's blue, it's present or it's absent.

Characteristics of Contrastive Attention to Detail

What it's About: Identification of individual elements or comparison to a known or present element or value.

Mantra: "It's either right or wrong."

Objective: There is only one solution.

No Specialized Knowledge Required: In general, no specialized knowledge is required for contrastive attention to detail. Specific skills or task-specific training may be appropriate.

Easy to Systematize: By nature, it is simple to create systems to minimize errors for tasks or processes requiring contrastive attention to detail. In many cases, a checklist or basic step-by-step procedure is adequate.

Some roles where contrastive attention to detail is important include:

- Administrative & clerical
- Sales & marketing
- Data entry
- Engineering
- Editing / Review
- Construction
- Production
- Quality control
- Accounting & bookkeeping
- Medical
- Lab & quality control

The short list above is far from all-inclusive. It's worth noting that every profession requires a great deal of contrastive attention to detail in some capacity. Contrastive attention to detail is typically the main concern for people trying to reduce or eradicate mistakes. It is certainly the reason for most of the calls and online inquiries I receive.

Analytical Attention to Detail

Most knowledge workers operate within the context of analytical attention to detail. Each day they do their best to identify the most important and/or relevant elements of a challenge or problem to combine and/or adjust them in order to bring about an appropriate solution -- at least for the moment. There are often multiple solutions, and the knowledge worker must apply judgement based on his or her knowledge and experience.

Characteristics of Analytical Attention to Detail

What it's About: Identifying the relevant *and irrelevant* elements of a problem or issue and applying knowledge to develop a solution.

Mantra: "There's a solution here."

It May Be Subjective: There are probably multiple possible solutions. While the desired end result may include precise specifications, there may be multiple solutions or possibilities for achieving it.

Specialized Knowledge Required: Specialized knowledge of the profession, field, or industry will be needed in order to identify the appropriate elements or develop an appropriate result. Specific skills or task-specific training may be appropriate.

Can Be Partially or Fully Systematized: Challenges requiring analytical attention to detail can be largely systematized by breaking them into contrastive elements. Generally, the final decision or prescribed action will require the application of specialized knowledge so systemization is primarily focused on increasing consistency of outcomes, reducing errors, and conserving resources.

There is a great deal of overlap between analytical and contrastive attention to detail with the main difference between the two being that analytical attention to detail is solution-oriented and there is often more than one solution.

The concept of "right or wrong" certainly applies but there may be more than one correct solution. Perhaps this is an over-simplification, but if you were given five identical sticks and told to make a shape with them in which each stick end is touching another end, you would probably make a pentagon or a five-pointed star and both would be correct solutions, given the instructions. Alternatively, if told to design an airplane wing that meets certain strength and speed requirements given certain aspects of the airplane to which they will be attached, there would undoubtedly be multiple (numerous) possible solutions. Obviously, in real life the problems and their solutions involve more variables than five sticks or even just a set of design specs. You may need to decide the "best" course of action for moving a company forward in the face of seemingly few opportunities and given several sets of constraints -- money, people, time, operational capacity, or all of these.

Roles where analytical attention to detail is important include:

- Research
- Law enforcement
- Real Estate
- Design & engineering
- Construction
- Production
- Lab roles
- Creative roles
- Investments
- Consulting
- Entrepreneurship
- Executive & management

Additive Attention to Detail

Additive attention to detail is what elicits complementary statements such as, "Their attention to detail is what makes them so great" or "Attention to detail is evident in everything they do." It is often about creating something people didn't even know they cared about until they've had it or experienced it.

A wide range of experiences and the skills and traits of observation and inquisitiveness, respectively, are often the main drivers behind creativity and innovation.[5] People with high levels of additive attention to detail are often revered because they generate inspiring ideas and create products and experiences beyond our expectations.

Characteristics of Additive Attention to Detail

For the person defining the required detail(s), the matter may be one of right vs. wrong. In reality, there are likely multiple -- or even endless -- solutions to achieve the desired result. Steve Jobs' attention to detail is legendary and his additive attention to detail is evident in the products whose development he led. The confidence he had in his vision and his "right or wrong" clarity probably seemed like a matter of contrastive attention to detail for the person(s) assigned to the project.

What it's About: Improvement. Innovation. Creating excellence.

Mantra: "Make it better." Contrary: never, "It's good enough."

---

[5] Sims, Peter. *LIttle Bets: How Breakthrough Ideas Emerge from Small Discoveries.* New York: Free Press, 2011.

Subjective: There may be endless "best" solutions, almost definitely more than one.

Specialized Knowledge Required: Specialized knowledge, extensive experience, mastery of the subject, and perhaps even insight and inspiration will help produce the best solutions to challenges requiring additive attention to detail.

Systematization of the Process: The nature of additive attention to detail is that something new -- an improvement or an innovation -- is being created. Because every time is a "first," systemization is somewhat difficult. However, the process of identifying the numerous contributory elements and the opportunities for improvement or innovation can be systematized.

Roles where additive attention to detail is important include:

- Inventors
- Creative roles
- Service
- Design roles
- Consulting
- Entrepreneur
- Leaders and executives

Systematizing Additive Attention to Detail

As previously mentioned, you cannot systematize an innovation, but you can create systems for the *development* of innovations, including how to identify opportunities for innovation.

Systems are designed to bring about a consistent conclusion or result so, by definition, a system will not bring around an innovation. Meaningful innovations should solve a problem, improve an experience, or capitalize on an opportunity. Systems can be designed, implemented, and managed to help ensure you identify and process the maximum number of elements that are relevant to the products, services, experiences, or systems you intend to improve.

In order to consistently identify opportunities for innovation, your system should facilitate a complete awareness of your current and potential markets, all current and potential products made by you *as well as* your competitors and current and upcoming technologies. You must be wholly aware of your market, how they use the products in question, what features they like, don't care about, hate, and so on. What technologies do you have in hand? Is there new, relevant technology on the horizon you could utilize? Additionally, your system needs to account for your current operational and strategic strengths and limitations. As each element is identified, there should be a system for researching and vetting that element. Each element should even be looked at from a historical perspective. Is it eerily similar to something that was tried before and didn't work? If so, is there a reason for that?

And this is just the start.

This may seem overly complicated. You may have been around or at least heard of organizations that were great at innovating because the scientists or engineers or whoever worked on the products were amazing and seemed to produce new products, ideas, or patents on an almost daily basis. Remember, part of the purpose of systemization is to remove the need for knowledge. With the proper system in place engineers don't have to be the only ones working on innovations; you can get everyone in the organization involved with innovation. With the proper system in place, you can innovate more consistently and prolifically.

Move Toward Contrastive

While many tasks or challenges are straightforwardly contrastive because they have only one solution -- a single element to identify or a single appropriate response -- most tasks or projects are more complex in nature.

Like most people, you probably operate in a world where you are trying to solve problems, big or small, throughout the day. You can reduce errors and create a more consistent outcome in any task or challenge -- especially repetitive ones -- by breaking it down into individual and more contrastive elements. You should always be looking for opportunities to make solutions more contrastive. By doing so, you remove the need for specialized knowledge and can enable systems that will essentially automate attention to detail, among other benefits.

The Basics of Attention

"Working is one of the most dangerous forms of procrastination." -- Gretchen Rubin

Attention is a complex concept we take for granted. We use our attentional resources almost constantly while awake, but are rarely conscious of them. I believe this is why managers, colleagues, and parents get frustrated when saying, "Be more detail-oriented" or "Pay attention!" to subordinates, colleagues, or children does not result in the desired improvement. While getting someone to "snap out of it" and be more alert certainly would help improve their attention to a given subject or task, it is unlikely to be adequate in producing sustainable improvement. There is simply more to it than that.

As a simple comparison, you eat food every day, but that does not mean I can expect you to take on the traits of an expert food taster by simply demanding that you "Taste more!" Doing so would definitely evoke from you more awareness about the food in your mouth, but it would do little or nothing to help you understand and be able to express the distinctive nuances of texture, types of taste, taste descriptions, and the other knowledge and skills experienced food tasters learn and hone over time. The reason this comparison works is because, just like there are people who appear to be naturally detail-oriented without giving the topic special consideration or gaining training, there are also people who are naturally better at distinguishing the complex and varied flavors, spices, and aromas in foods. We'll leave the "nature vs. nurture" discussion for another time.

Anyone who wants to improve their attention to detail and learn its fundamentals needs to understand the important aspects of attention. A general understanding of what I call "the basics of attention" will help you on your path to becoming a more aware, focused, accurate, and overall more detail-oriented person.

4 Aspects of Attention

The topic of attention is exceptionally complex. It is even somewhat of an enigma for scientists and practitioners in the fields of behavioral psychology and cognitive research. Some of them even joke that not even they truly know what attention is.[6] Fortunately, we only need a basic understanding of attention in order to create a strong foundation for understanding how to improve attention to detail. So, let's start with these 4 main aspects of attention - - Orientation/Direction, Selection/Omission, Sustainability, and Executive Function.

---

[6] Boaz, Ben David. *"Attention: Cognitive Psychology".* Teaching Innovation Unit - IDC, 25 Dec. 2014, www.youtube.com/watch?v=bRej7Ak-QBA.

Orientation / Direction

The first clear thing about attention is that it can be oriented, or directed, to attend to various stimuli. Sometimes it is directed deliberately and thoughtfully, while other times it is carelessly thrown around at whatever moves next or makes the loudest noise.

Orientation is our most basic component of attention; it is essentially instinctual. It is a basic awareness of the physical objects, threats, or ideas around you (physically or cognitively). If you want a basic awareness of every item or concern in your physical or mental environment, then orientation is all you need. However, if you need to get something done -- to focus on completing one task or on effectively handling a single issue -- the other elements of attention are required.

Selection / Omission

The second critical aspect of attention is that it can be both focused and suppressed, as needed, to help us more efficiently operate within our environment -- and these actions can happen simultaneously.[7] From an evolutionary standpoint, the development of this ability is about survival. It is what enabled our ancestors to selectively attend to the rustling sound in the brush -- listening, looking, and even smelling for the distinct cues from impending predators -- while simultaneously suppressing attention to things that didn't matter such as fluttering birds' wings, scurrying rodents, and the wind in the leaves.

In today's world, this instinctual ability -- albeit weak in most of us -- is what enables us to focus on (selectively attend to) the important, deadline-driven task at hand while ignoring (omitting) the rings and buzzes from our cell

---

[7] Gazzaley, Adam and Larry D. Rosen. *The Distracted Mind: Ancient Brains in a High-Tech World*. MIT Press, 2016.

phones, water cooler conversations, and other unimportant stimuli.

Sustainability

And then we have sustainability, which is our ability to keep our attention focused upon a specific object or stimuli. Without sustainability, we wouldn't be able to get many things done. We would constant switch from one activity to the next and never get much at all accomplished.

Executive Function

The executive function is the management division of our attention. Orientation/Direction, Selection/Omission, and Sustainability are the workers, but are not very efficient or effective without proper management. Executive function provides guidance, decisions, and willpower to keep the other parts of our attention working together smoothly and moving in the same general direction. It is also the most resource-hungry component of attention.

Attention is a Limited Resource

Understanding the fact that attention is a limited resource is one of the most important components of becoming a more detail-oriented person.

I am all about keeping things simple and focused, which is why this book is so short. If you want more technical and certainly more physiologically-detailed descriptions of how the brain works as it relates to attention, I suggest you read David Rock's *Your Mind at Work* and/or Adam Gazzaley and Larry D. Rosen's *The Distracted Mind*. Both books have certainly influenced me and are excellent resources if you want to delve more deeply into how the brain works.

Interruptions and Distractions (Interference)

A brief discussion of interruptions and distractions might help make several of the upcoming topics easier to follow and even more interesting. Simply put:

A **distraction** is a stimulus that pulls at your attention and/or prevents concentration on the task at hand *but does not require you to stop the task*.

An **interruption** is a distraction *you've actively engaged* **and shifted your attention or concentration** toward.

For example, let's say you are working on a current-quarter sales report for an upcoming meeting. You are concentrating reasonably well until a pair of co-workers starts chatting about the next quarter's goals several feet away. The topic might be interesting to you, but is not entirely relevant. It is a distraction. While you continue working on your report, your attention is now fragmented between the report you are working on and their conversation. You hear bits and pieces of what they are saying until something really catches your interest so you stop working on the report -- an interruption -- and ask them to "repeat that last part".

Whether you asked them to repeat the last part or asked them to go have their conversation somewhere else, the coworkers still became an interruption *because you engaged them*; you stopped what you were doing to address the distraction.

Both distractions and interruptions can be internal or external. Internal distractions are your thoughts. They might include thoughts about your next vacation, a dying pet, your weekend hobby, or even work when you should be focusing on your child's homework.

These distractions become interruptions when you stop what you are doing to attend to them -- to get a price for plane tickets, check with the vet, look up tee times, or peek at email. External distractions come from outside yourself. Examples include noisy coworkers, a leaky faucet, a bird squawking in the tree outside your window, a child who asks a question every 37 seconds, or any other external stimulus that breaks your concentration on the task at hand.

Your Attentional Battery

A battery stores chemical energy which it turns into electricity on demand.

Think of your brain as having a rechargeable "attention battery" and the attention that battery stores is what powers your *focus*. Just like a regular battery, your attention battery can be used efficiently or inefficiently. Efficient use of the battery can make it last significantly longer -- enabling you to sustain an effective level of focus and a higher level of attention to detail.

Smartphones present a good -- and reasonably relevant -- analogy. To start, you are probably aware that some apps use significantly more energy than others. Playing a graphic-intensive, online game will run down your phone's battery much faster than playing something simpler such as solitaire or Sudoku. You also know you can conserve energy by dimming the screen slightly when you are using it, and by turning off apps you are not using instead of allowing them to run in the background.

You can essentially say the same things about your brain's attention battery. Some tasks require more attention than others in order to focus effectively. You can conserve attention by applying it more efficiently and, ideally, you should apply it to only one task at a time instead of leaving distractions active around you (like apps running in the background).

The difference between your smartphone's battery and your attention battery is that your attention battery needs to be kept fairly full in order to generate effective levels of focus whereas your cell phone will continue to operate normally until the last bit of energy has been spent and the phone shuts down.

Your attention can be depleted and it can be replenished. Likewise, it can be wasted and it can be conserved. It can be spent wisely or unwisely, efficiently or inefficiently.

It can also be recharged. Unfortunately, recharging your attention is not as simple as plugging in. Ironically, we sometimes affectionately refer to most of the ways we recharge attention (and mental energy in general) as "*un*plugging".

Spending & Recharging Attention

Just as a bright screen and large, complex apps are especially draining on a phone's battery, certain processes and activities are especially draining on your attentional resources.

Activities that Drain Attention

The following activities, issues, or processes can inflict significant strain on your attentional resources, leading to a decrease in your ability to focus at an optimal level (in no particular order):

- Decision making
- Distractions and interruptions
- Worry / Anxiety (related to distractions & interruptions but are important enough to warrant a separate mention)
- Task-switching (aka: Multi-tasking)

- Physiological impairment (hunger, lack of sleep, drugs or alcohol, illness)
- Prioritizing[8]
- Impulse control

---

[8] Rock, David. *Your Brain at Work: Strategies for Overcoming Distraction, Regaining Focus and Working Smarter All Day Long.* Harper Collins, 2010.

Activities that Recharge Attention

The following activities have been shown, through research, to recharge attentional resources:

- Relaxing breaks (walks, exposure to nature, daydreaming, reading fiction)[9]
- Sleep, including naps
- Light exercise -- Citation

---

[9] Gazzaley, Adam and Larry D. Rosen. *The Distracted Mind: Ancient Brains in a High-Tech World*. MIT Press, 2016.

- Meditation -- Citation
- Light, healthy snack

Ways to Optimize Attention

At first, you might just think, "Got it, minimize the things listed on the 'attention drainers' list" -- and that is a good start -- *but you can do better than that*. You can conserve and optimize your attentional resources using two main tactics.

First, you can use deliberate and conscientious methods of time and task management. Second, you should engage in the right kinds of activities before starting your day or entering into any task, project, or endeavor. Doing the right things -- essentially the definition of being effective -- can significantly improve and extend your ability to sustain your attention on individual tasks which will directly improve your overall accuracy and productivity.

Here are three methods effective people use to optimize attentional resources and their overall effectiveness:

1. Invest in Planning & Prioritizing

Planning and prioritizing (decision-making activities) are resource hungry, mentally speaking. They are, however, required in order to effectively perform any project or set of tasks.

Unfortunately, the vast majority of people do not adequately invest in planning and prioritizing before starting their day or even some complex projects. The result is that after tasks are completed -- tasks which no doubt drained some amount of energy from their attentional batteries -- they have to spend time deciding what other tasks need to be performed (planning) *and* which task to complete *next* (prioritizing). That time between tasks, even when just a few minutes, would be more effectively used by taking a quick walk, meditating, or even doodling on a blank piece of paper. Instead, they dive into those attention draining activities of planning and prioritizing before starting their next attention draining task.

By operating your day or a project on a plan-as-you-go model, you are essentially adding a layer of task-switching between everything you do. It is well known that there is a sort of "setup cost" involved with starting any new task. Even answering the phone in the middle of a task means you're going to have a "Now, where was I?" moment when you get off the phone. The same mental process happens every time you move from one task to another. You cannot entirely avoid it but you can greatly minimize it.

Given that planning, prioritizing, and task-switching are all attention draining activities, we should do what we can to minimize the number of times we do them repeatedly throughout the day.

Plan & Prioritize First To Maximize Cognitive Resources

Five Tasks Completed With & Without Initial Planning & Prioritizing

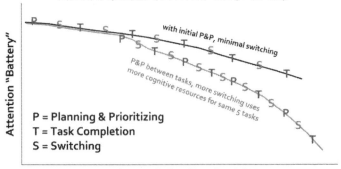

P = Planning & Prioritizing
T = Task Completion
S = Switching

Task Completion / Productivity

To avoid this completely inefficient expenditure of your attentional resources, invest adequate time in planning and prioritizing before starting your day or before launching into a project. Focusing on planning and prioritizing all at once requires significantly less energy than the cumulative energy used when you repeatedly conduct the "What should I do next?" routine. When your day or project is properly planned *and* your task items (your to-dos) are clearly prioritized, you can simply complete a task and smoothly move on to the next task without the additional layer of task-switching. The decision has already been made. You overachievers might even want to plan what you will do during your relaxing breaks.

2. Do the Most Important (or Difficult) Tasks First

Most people leave the most difficult tasks of their day for last and that gives them an excellent opportunity at the end of the day to put the task off until tomorrow. Doing this is mentally draining in two ways. First, procrastination can create a significant amount of anxiety because you know the task needs to be done and putting it off often exacerbates a stressful situation because of a looming deadline or potential loss of opportunity. Second, the habit of procrastination leaves yet another item on your already cluttered mental plate. It's just another item to come back to again and again, wasting time and mental resources each time you deal with it.

The trap of pushing off the most difficult tasks is easy when there are numerous low value tasks to be done. We convince ourselves that we are busy and just ran out of time because, after all, there is a complete list of to-do's checked off our list at the end of the day. In many cases, we would have been as productive -- or more -- if the single important item was completed and we quit working before lunch. Instead, we toil away at the low-value items while leaving the big, daunting tasks for tomorrow.

By putting more difficult and/or important tasks first, you set yourself up for a day that is "all downhill from there." The tough problem is solved. The hard part is done, stress and anxiety are largely gone, and the rest of the day can be accomplished without the burden or pressure of something you want to avoid, even if only subconsciously.

So, while you are planning and prioritizing, make sure to put the toughest and/or most important items first. In short, "Get it done!"

3. Stop Multi-Tasking: It's actually "Task-Switching"

If you have spent much time reviewing resumes you have seen how many people like to include "multi-tasking" as one of their skills or abilities. This is only anecdotal, but it appears that the younger a person is, the more likely they are to include "multi-tasking" on their resume -- probably because someone told them it is a desirable trait (and it is, in theory).

The fact is people are not good at multi-tasking. The results of studies are quite clear that when people try to do two complex tasks at once they end up doing both much less effectively. David E. Meyer, PhD clarifies that the mental blocks created by switching between tasks can cost as much as 40 percent of a person's productive time.[10] This makes perfect sense when you look at how the brain works. Cognitively, "multi-tasking" is not truly possible. The part of the brain largely responsible for complex tasks -- the frontal lobe and, more specifically, the prefrontal cortex -- simply does not do two things at one time. It performs one task and then *switches* to the other. If you insist on trying to do two things at once, then the brain is simply applying attentional resources to one task and then *switching* attention to the other task, and back and forth, and so on. It does not matter how much you try. Consider how much opportunity this leaves for making mistakes.

---

[10] "Multitasking: switching costs". www.apa.org, http://www.apa.org/research/action/multitask.aspx. Accessed 8/15/2018.

You will make fewer mistakes, be more creative, and more productive if you focus all your cognitive resources on one complex task and then move on to the next. It's ok to chew gum.

Summary:

- Prioritize first[11]
- Do the most important tasks first
- Do one thing at a time

---

[11] Rock, David. *Your Brain at Work: Strategies for Overcoming Distraction, Regaining Focus and Working Smarter All Day Long.* Harper Collins, 2010.

The 5 Fundamentals of Attention to Detail

There are five fundamental elements of attention to detail.

These five fundamentals, or *really* the lack of considering them, are at the root of why there is often frustration around attention to detail. The concept of "attention to detail" is commonly used ambiguously. We are quick to say, "Pay more attention to detail" or "Be more detail-oriented" to a colleague or employee (or spouse or child) who has made a mistake that could have been avoided with what we simply label as a lack of attention to detail. Here's the thing: what we think of as -- or *realize* as -- relevant details (i.e. elements, issues, items, ideas, etc.) may not be so obvious to the person with whom we are frustrated. Or, perhaps he simply lacks the same level of interest or knowledge we have in the subject matter. Or, perhaps the *goal* of the task or the *reason it is important* to perform it a certain way or perform at a certain level is unclear.

Consider these five fundamental elements of attention to detail so that next time you feel like saying, "Be more detail-oriented" or "Pay more attention to detail" you will have something more specific to add. In fact, after reading this chapter, you will probably conclude that it may be more appropriate to ask a few questions and say something more along the lines of, "I think we may improve your results with a little more training in..." or "The outcome we're trying to achieve here is…" or "Your role in this task is important because…"

The relevance of each fundamental element depends upon the task at hand, the intended results, the types of attention to detail most important to you, and your level of competence with the task or subject. The fundamental elements can complement or offset one another based on your current aptitude with, and/or openness to, each of them as they relate to the task at hand. For example, if you are exceptionally knowledgeable about a specific task, for whatever reason, but are generally distracted at the moment (i.e., demonstrating minimal focus) and have little interest in the topic, you may still be able to exhibit a high degree of attention to detail in the matter simply because of your experience, education, and/or training related to the task.

The five fundamental elements of attention to detail are:

- Focus
- Knowledge
- Interest
- Systems
- RoW attitude

Let's look more closely at each element and the various components of each.

Focus

Focus is the broadest and, probably, the most obvious element of attention to detail. Without sustained and appropriately intense focus, our attention to any task or subject -- and its details -- will be inadequate.

The components of focus as it relates to attention to detail include:

- Mindfulness
- Process-orientation
- Environment
- Physiology

If you want to develop strong, well-rounded attention to detail, you need to improve and facilitate an effective level of focus. It can be improved through *practice* and supported -- or hindered -- by your actions and environment. I should clarify that it is not the most *important* element of attention to detail, but I consider it a critical component of developing a strong *general* foundation that will help you in any scenario.

Mindfulness

One of the practices I have enjoyed most during my research and studies of attention and how to become more detail-oriented is the discovery of mindfulness and meditation. I've never been one to be interested in things some might categorize under "holistic" or "Eastern philosophies" or maybe even humorously as "hippie stuff" but my earliest research quickly revealed that mindfulness is requisite to attention to detail, so I was compelled to delve into it. To my surprise, it was a life-changing discovery.

In fact, I am disappointed that the topic is thought of by so many as being foreign, intimidating, or even "new age". I liken it to the general attitude toward wine in the United States before the early 2000's when there was something of a wine revolution led by people like Gary Vaynerchuk and his raw, down-to-earth approach to wine education. Before that, wine was intimidating for many people and, literally, kind of *foreign*. There was a feeling that if you bought a bottle of wine, you were supposed to know something about grapes and regions of the world and be able to pronounce the name correctly. Then, people started realizing that wine is just another drink. It's delicious, fun, and anyone can enjoy it -- without feeling awkward about it. People suddenly became much more comfortable with trying it. Just because someone else likes a wine, doesn't mean you have to like it too! Between 2000 and 2016, the United States went from being the world's third largest consumer of wine -- behind France and Italy -- to being the top consumer of wine. A similar kind of revolution is happening for mindfulness meditation, and I am happy about it.

It's About Awareness

Mindfulness training is about teaching yourself to be more aware, present, and focused.[12] That is *my summary* of the definition provided by Tessa Watt, a UK-based mindfulness trainer and consultant in her book *Mindfulness: A Practical Guide* (my favorite on the subject). You could quickly find more complicated descriptions and definitions of mindfulness, but I like this one because it keeps the concept of mindfulness simple and unintimidating. To me, it is the definition most appropriate for anyone who wants to improve mindfulness but has yet to develop an interest in studying the topic deeply. It is also the most relevant version for the topic of improving attention to detail.

Benefits of Meditation

Numerous studies have been conducted on the benefits of meditation. Research consistently demonstrates that mindfulness meditation makes a

---

[12] Watt, Tessa. Mindfulness: A Practical Guide. MJF Books, 2012.

positive impact on attitude, stress levels, workplace performance, job satisfaction, and even health. Health insurance provider Aetna reported that employees' average productivity increased by about $3,000 per year after participating in a mindfulness training program.[13]

To capitalize on benefits like these, a growing number of large companies offer meditation programs to their employees, including:

- Apple
- Google
- Nike
- AOL Time Warner
- McKinsey & Co.
- Yahoo!
- Deutsche Bank
- Proctor & Gamble
- HBO[14]
- Aetna
- General Mills

---

[13] Kim, Hannah H. "The Meditation Industry.", *sagepub.com*, http://businessresearcher.sagepub.com/sbr-1946-105603-2878495/20180129/the-meditation-industry. Accessed 6/30/2018
[14] "10 Big Companies that Promote Employee Meditation." *Sonorrari.com*, https://www.sonorrari.com/single-post/2017/04/06/10-Big-Companies-That-Promote-Employee-Meditation. Accessed 6/30/2018.

- Intel
- Target
- Green Mountain Coffee Roasters[15]

That list is just a handful of big, recognizable companies and is far from all-inclusive. The number of companies adding mindfulness training programs is rapidly increasing. A 2017 survey by Fidelity Investments and the National Business Group on Health concluded that 35 percent of responding employers had incorporated mindfulness training in the workplace and another 26 percent were considering adding it in the future.[16]

Practicing Mindfulness

Here's the first thing you need to know about meditation: Your mind *will* drift -- and that is natural.

If you are even a little experienced with meditation you already know this.

In fact, practicing ignoring those drifting thoughts is essentially *the point* of meditation. There is a broad

---

[15] Schaufenbuel, Kimberly. "Why Google, Target, and General Mills Are Investing in Mindfulness." *hbr.org*, https://hbr.org/2015/12/why-google-target-and-general-mills-are-investing-in-mindfulness. Accessed 6/30/2018.

[16] Kim, Hannah H. "The Meditation Industry." *sagepub.com*, http://businessresearcher.sagepub.com/sbr-1946-105603-2878495/20180129/the-meditation-industry. Accessed 6/30/2018

consensus that this is the #1 frustration for people learning meditation. They get relaxed, find their focus (on their breath, a sound, whatever), and are doing great -- so relaxed, in the moment, at peace -- and then they suddenly realize they've been thinking about an issue at work or the kids' schedule or what they should have said to the rude attendant at the oil change place. Drifting off IS NORMAL. The key to successful meditation is learning to recognize when you've drifted and calmly bring your thoughts back to your intended focus.

Entire books are written on the topic of meditation, so I'm keeping the coverage here light and to the bare minimum. If you want to delve further into the topic -- and you will be glad you did -- I suggest you start with *Mindfulness: A Practical Guide* by Tessa Watt. It's an easy read with simple exercises to try as you go. You might also try an app such as *Calm* (my personal favorite), which is available for Android and iPhone devices. If you want to start with an app, I definitely suggest reading at least a little about meditation to develop a better understanding of breathing techniques and posture as well as a general appreciation for the various methods and applications.

Here's How I Meditate

I merely practice the art of meditation. I am not a meditation instructor at the time of this writing, so it is simply not appropriate for me to provide instructions on how to meditate. However, I am completely comfortable sharing *how I meditate*. Borrow from it, ignore it, or enhance it with your own preferences and/or professional instruction.

I mediate sitting or lying down. Seventy-five percent of the time I use the Calm app, listen to classical music (Beethoven's Moonlight Sonata on repeat is my favorite) probably 15 percent of the time, or I simply enjoy the silence if I'm in a particularly calming or quiet place (10 percent).

Sitting Meditation: When sitting, I prefer a comfortable, padded chair. The average office or "executive" chair works great because I can easily maintain a fairly straight posture and the cushioning is soft enough to relax but supportive enough that I don't "sink in" like on a couch. I keep my back straight, but relaxed, and my shoulders comfortably rolled back so I'm not slouching. Both of my feet are on the floor and my hands are relaxed. I lay one on each thigh or maybe put them together over my lap. I close my eyes and focus my attention either on my breathing -- each detail of it -- or I "stare at" a point in space (this really only works if the room is completely dark). My sitting meditations are usually about five minutes long.

Occasionally, if I am at a particularly comfortable place such as a quiet beach or a gym with an unoccupied studio, I sit on the floor or on a pillow with my legs crossed.

Lying Meditation: I often meditate with the intention of falling asleep at some point. In this case, I lie flat with no pillow (I don't usually sleep with a pillow as I find they cause neck pain), and my arms at my sides. When lying down, I usually set the timer on the Calm app for 25 minutes. My favorite sleep meditation on the Calm app is the "Deep Sleep Release" session but they have many great sessions. Frankly, I have no idea how far I get into the 25-minute session before falling asleep, but my guess is that it is in the 10 to 15-minute range on average.

I usually do 5 or 10-minute sessions because this is enough for my purposes. I simply want to take a break, clear my mind, improve my focus, and generally relax. When I first started meditation, five minutes was nearly impossible for me. My sessions then were one or two minutes and even now, on particularly stressful days when there is an especially large workload or extra chaos, I find it hard to maintain my focus for more than a few minutes. It is those times when I am most reminded that the point of meditation is to practice bringing myself back into a mindful state -- back into focus. **Mindfulness is essentially the practice of ignoring distractions and that, I believe, is why it is so effective for helping to improve focus, attention to detail, and overall productivity.** On most days, however, I am surprised at how short five minutes feels, so I do a second session. I have talked to people -- regular people, not "gurus" or meditation experts -- who meditate for up to an hour. That fascinates me and makes wonder me what I might experience if I achieve that level of meditation. For now, my meditation practice serves my purpose effectively. There may be people who read this and send me an email to tell me I'm doing it wrong. My response? We may not agree on wines, either. And, that's my point. Your meditation practice should be something that serves you and that you enjoy.

Control Your Environment

Controlling, or at least optimizing, your environment is an essential component of focus. Here are some ways you can improve your ability to control your environment in the real world.

Value your time: Be clear with yourself about the value of your time and how you use it. Mindfulness plays a role in this because you need a certain level of awareness of yourself and what you were doing in order to recognize that you are not using your time as effectively as possible. At least as important is to make sure you are managing how other people affect your time.

Learn to say "no" or "later": We have all been deep into our work when someone enters our office or even throws a file on our desk and says, "Hey, take a look at this" or "What do you think about...?"

In most cases it is completely reasonable for you to tell a coworker something to the effect of, "I'm almost done with what I'm working on and want to keep my head in it. I'll come find you in 10 minutes" or "Give me 30 minutes to finish what I'm doing here so I can give full attention to this."

The hierarchical structure of your workplace is certainly something to consider, so if your boss is the one interrupting you, then you may have to use a different message or even stop what you're doing and go with it.

Tip: If this kind of interruption is common for you then create some kind of system that helps you easily pick up where you left off faster and easier. A notepad or sticky note may be adequate.

Learning to say "later" is especially hard for people who tend to be more amiable and agreeable, but learning to do it effectively can make you more productive and can even decrease stress levels because you were taking more control over your work and time.

Get rid of desk and computer clutter: Keep your work area free of distractions. This applies to your desk or workbench, shelves, and even your computer.

There are numerous brilliant and productive people whose desks are perpetually messy. The simple fact, though, is that a cluttered desk provides dozens of opportunities for distractions every day. Make cleaning your desk a habit. I even include it on my list of to-do items two or three days each week and typically find that about half of the papers in the stack belong in the trash.

Keep your computer free of clutter, too. By far the most common application for this is browser tabs. As a recovering browser tab abuser I can tell you first hand that closing the tabs you aren't going to use for a while is liberating. Your computer will run better, too. There was a time when you could have walked up to my computer and seen as many as 60 browser tabs open (yeah, crazy, I know). They were all tabs I *intended* to come back to at some point but if the browser crashed or the computer restarted for an update and I lost all the tabs I never cared. Yet, I still had that habit.

Now, the tabs I keep open in my browser are based on my to-do list. On a busy day I might have 10 or 12 tabs open. After correcting this habit my computer runs better, I spend less time clicking around browser tabs trying to find the one I was on before, and there are no tempting distractions from useless tabs with articles, Facebook, email, or anything else I'm not going to be working on within a few hours.

The concept and mindset are the same for your desk and your browser tabs. Simply be honest about what you need to be there and get rid of the rest.

Turn off notifications: every app on your phone -- and the company behind it -- is vying for your attention throughout the day. They want to remind you or alert you about something -- news, new friend requests, friend request accepted, text messages, voicemails, push notifications, available upgrades, new products, comments on forums and blogs and posts, tweets, snaps, and so on.

And, like Pavlov's dogs, we react to the commands. We look to see what's going on or at least slap at our pocket to see if that was actually a vibration we felt or just a phantom vibration -- because phantom vibrations are a real thing now.

Turn off all the notifications on your phone. Only look at it when you feel like looking at it. The phantom vibrations will eventually go away and you will have a renewed sense of control over your device.

Control noise: Do what you can to minimize any noise that pulls at your attention.

There are hundreds of possible scenarios for a noisy office environment. You may have to deal with people chatting in the cubicle next to you, coworkers who talk loudly on the phone, a desk mate who likes to click his pen, bosses or coworkers who like to stop by your desk regularly, or maybe you just sit close to the water cooler.

Whatever your particular situation, you might be able to solve it by simply and tactfully asking someone to "Keep it down", by moving your desk, working in a meeting or conference room sometimes, closing your office door, wearing headphones, or by moving the water cooler.

Many people swear that they are more productive when listening to music; and this may be true. The caveat I would like you to consider is that you should listen to music that does not have words. Music with words -- even songs you "know by heart" because you've heard them a thousand times -- pulls at your involuntary attention and essentially subconsciously distracts you from fully focusing on the task at hand because part of your mental energy is spent thinking about the words. Classical music, light jazz, natural sounds (rain, flowing river, thunderstorms) or even "white noise" are great options. Various research indicates that the ideal speed for optimizing focus is somewhere around 60 beats per minute.

Be Process-Oriented Versus Outcome-Focused

Excellent outcomes are achieved by the conscientious execution of the individual steps or components you must complete in order to reach the outcome.

The best artisans and athletes tend to operate with a process-oriented focus. This is the essence of sayings about achievements such as reaching the top of the mountain happening one step at a time. Professional marathon runners may mention focusing on the individual steps to the finish line. Incidentally, the "steps" may also include persistent practice, meticulous attention to diet, breathing exercises, visualization, and more. The best quilts are made one patch or even one stitch at a time.

The book *The 4 Disciplines of Execution* by Chris McChesney, Sean Covey, and Jim Huling gives what I believe is the best business-related context for the concept of being process-oriented. Their discussion of driving results via lead metrics captures the essence of how you should drive a process-oriented culture to achieve big goals in a company.

Lead metrics[17] are the measurable steps you can take to achieve a desired outcome. For example, if you want to reach $100,000 in sales each month, you should calculate how many phone calls and customer visits need to be made per day -- maybe even per hour -- to achieve that level of sales. Then, focus on executing your daily goals -- on the lead metrics -- with excellence. The sales will come.

You can apply the concept of lead metrics to anything. The concept and process works for anything from improving your long game (hit 20/30/50 balls per day) to losing weight (ignore the scale and eat only X calories per day) to improving the customer experience (find one thing to improve every day) to making more friends (say hello to and/or give a compliment to one new person each day) to reducing the number of

---

[17] McChesney, Chris., Covey, Sean., Huling, Jim. *The 4 Disciplines Of Execution: Achieving Your Wildly Important Goals*. New York: Free Press, 2012. Print.

errors you make in spreadsheets (verify or double check every column twice). You can apply the concept to anything. Try it.

Physiology

A healthy body makes for a stronger mind. Overall, it's a good idea to manage how you treat your body and what you put into it. Science has proven this repeatedly, and you probably even have personal experience that supports it.

Your Brain Uses a Lot of Energy

Your brain is a resource-intensive organ. In fact, it uses approximately 20 percent of the body's total energy requirement.[18] The chapter in this book about attention covers your cognitive resources more effectively so here we will stick to how you can affect and/or improve your brain's function physiologically. In short, though, keep in mind that your brain uses more energy (exponentially more) when learning new tasks or during critical thinking than when performing simple or repeated tasks. Your brain becomes more efficient

---

[18] Swaminathan, Nikhil. *"Why Does The Brain Need So Much Power?"*. ScientificAmerican.com, https://www.scientificamerican.com/article/why-does-the-brain-need-s/. Accessed 6/30/2018.

at performing tasks as you repeat them and gain mastery of a skill[19] or concept. Practice makes perfect.

To keep your focus and overall attention to detail sharp, there are exercises you can do and choices you can make to help your brain work more efficiently today -- almost immediately -- and for the long term.

For now, just remember: healthy body, healthy mind.

Stretching & Light Exercise Breaks

A brief stretch session or walk gets blood flowing and helps improve focus for the task at hand. I start many mornings with a simple morning routine I pieced together from time with a personal coach, yoga instruction, and books. On most mornings, I spend two to three minutes on the "routine." It wakes me up; gets my blood flowing a little; stretches my back, arms, and legs; and eliminates soreness and lower-back discomfort which I've been plagued with most mornings of my adult life regardless of mattresses and exercise levels.

---

[19] Messier, Claude and Beland-Miller, Alexandria. *"Does The Brain Use More Energy During Particular Activities?"*. Scientific American. https://www.scientificamerican.com/article/does-the-brain-use-more-energy-during-particular-activities/ Accessed 7/1/2018.

A morning session is a great way to start the day in the right direction, but short breaks of light exercise throughout the day are best to sustain strong cognitive function. Five minutes is adequate. You can even combine it with mindfulness and meditation.

A McMaster University study of university students demonstrated the benefits of light exercise breaks on learning and retention. Three groups of students watched a 50-minute online lecture. During the lecture, two of the groups took three five-minute breaks. The third group, the control, took no breaks. One of the two break-taking groups spent their breaks doing light calisthenics while the other spent their break time playing video games. All three groups were tested during the lecture to measure how well they were paying attention. They were also measured multiple times afterward to determine how well they retained the information they learned.

As you may have already guessed, the light exercise group came out significantly ahead of the other two groups. Their attention was more focused during the lecture, they retained more information immediately after and 48 hours afterward, and they "gave higher ratings for narrator clarity and perceived understanding" than the other two groups.[20]

Countless studies demonstrate similar benefits. Short bursts of light exercise deliver immediate cognitive benefits. Another study of college students tested their cognitive performance after 30 minutes on a treadmill. Participants demonstrated more effective allocation of cognitive resources "suggesting that acute bouts of cardiovascular exercise may facilitate improved allocation of attentional and memory resources and thereby improved executive function."[21]

Take occasional breaks to move around a little. It's good for your brain and helps you perform better.

Regular Exercise Changes the Brain

Research on the effects of exercise on the brain repeatedly demonstrates that just about any kind of exercise is good for the brain in some way. Regular

---

[20] DiSalvo, David. *"Short Bursts of Exercise Can Give Your Brain an Edge, Study Suggests."* Forbes.com, https://www.forbes.com/sites/daviddisalvo/2018/04/22/how-taking-short-exercise-breaks-can-give-your-brain-an-edge/#62ad14126fb2. Accessed 7/1/2018.

[21] Hogan, Candice L., Matta, Jutta., and Carstensen, Laura L. *"Exercise Holds Immediate Benefits for Affect and Cognition in Younger and Older Adults."* Ncbi.nlm.nih.gov, https://www.ncbi.nlm.nih.gov/pmc/articles/PMC3768113/. Accessed 7/1/2018.

exercise helps improve learning, thinking, and memory by essentially helping those regions of the brain grow.

Numerous studies have suggested that the prefrontal cortex and medial temporal cortex (areas involved in thinking and memory) have greater volume in people who exercise versus those who do not. Researchers in a study at the University of British Columbia found that *regular* aerobic exercise -- enough to get sweat going -- increases the size of the hippocampus, an area of the brain involved in learning and memory.[22]

A study led by Yorgi Mavros of Sydney University showed that strength training leads to improved cognitive function even in aging populations. His study included 100 people aged 55 to 86 who followed an exercise regime of twice-weekly weight training sessions. They lifted weights that were 80 percent of the maximum amount they could handle. Tests and MRI scans were used to measure the effects on their brains. Participants showed improved cognitive function and growth in key areas of their brains.[23]

---

[22] Godman, Heidi. *"Regular exercise changes the brain to improve memory, thinking skills."* Health.Harvard.Edu, https://www.health.harvard.edu/blog/regular-exercise-changes-brain-improve-memory-thinking-skills-201404097110. Accessed 6/30/2018

[23] Stillman, Jessica. "This Specific Type of Exercise Will Keep Your Brain Young, Study Says". Inc.com, https://www.inc.com/jessica-

What You Put Into Your Body Matters

The topics of Diet & Nutrition and Drugs & Alcohol are beyond the scope of this book; especially when we're all completely surrounded with information and advice about what we should and should not eat or drink.

Eat healthy, whatever that means to you. In general, research on nutrition says that just about any diet composed largely (it's ok to indulge sometimes) of fresh, natural, unprocessed foods with a reasonably well-balanced combination of proteins, fats, carbohydrates, vitamins, and nutrients is good for you and your brain. Feed your body and brain healthy food. Healthy food will energize and facilitate cognitive resources, while unhealthy foods (such as those high in refined sugars) can impair brain function and even worsen symptoms of depression[24] and anxiety.

---

stillman/this-specific-type-of-exercise-will-keep-your-brain-young-study-says.html. Accessed 6/30/2018.

[24] Selhub, Eva, MD. *"Nutritional psychiatry: Your brain on food."* Health.Harvard.edu, https://www.health.harvard.edu/blog/nutritional-psychiatry-your-brain-on-food-201511168626. Accessed 7/1/2018.

Knowledge

There are three components of knowledge:

- Education
- Training
- Experience

As it relates to attention to detail, knowledge boils down to knowing what to look for, what is relevant to your challenge or problem at hand, and what to include and/or exclude. Whether you are writing an email, fixing a water heater, completing a legal immigration document for a client, diagnosing a patient's illness, or building a spaceship, knowledge of one degree or another will come into play.

Some level of knowledge is assumed for certain tasks. That is, there is a basic competency for performing the task. For instance, an adult who works in an office-setting would generally be considered competent enough to create and send a reasonably coherent email, even if you know nothing else about that individual. Of course, to minimize or all together avoid errors in the email, the employee will be more successful if he is especially proficient with spelling and grammar and also knows something about the subject of the email. If a person is a medical doctor, she has undoubtedly been educated and trained in human physiology, medicine, and diagnostics among meeting the numerous other requirements of becoming a doctor. While the professional *experience* of an individual physician may be more than that of another, *incompetence* in this particular profession is fundamentally unacceptable and so education, testing, and training requirements have been developed to ensure a minimum level of knowledge. The more seasoned doctor's experience in diagnosis and treatment helps him or her catch subtle cues in how the patient describes his symptoms that a less experienced doctor may not catch without consulting one or more resources (journals, conference notes, other doctors).

Spaceship builders need to take advantage of dozens disciplines of education, training, and experience to tackle the exceptionally complex process of designing and building a spaceship -- especially the first of its kind. Once the spaceship design has been tested, corrected, and retested multiple times (an exceptional process of knowledge-building in itself) a sophisticated system of rules, checklists, procedures, and manuals can be developed to guide the construction of additional spaceships without the constraints of needing so many highly educated people to address concerns and develop solutions for each step of the construction process.

Education

Education is foundational and often largely theoretical. While lacking in practical application, the primary value of education is developing an awareness and understanding of the elements, history, and even the possibilities (theoretical) of an industry, profession, skill, or area of interest.

Education is typically our launching point for starting something new, for developing a new skill, and for rolling into the process of gaining practical training and experience to develop well-rounded knowledge over time. Depending on the field, profession, work, or task, the amount of education could be as short as several bullet points or as long as years of study.

Training

Training is the hands-on component of learning and developing knowledge. It's about developing specific skills or abilities -- or about learning *how to* develop them. We take part in training throughout our lives and different professions commonly use or require various levels of training through internships, apprenticeships, classes, labs, institutions, or on the job training.

Experience

Experience is developed with time, repetition, and exposure to a variety of scenarios where education and training are applied in real-world applications. It is arguably the most valuable type of knowledge by far because an experienced person has often "seen it all" -- or, has at least seen *most of it* before -- and can quickly identify the relevant elements of an issue or challenge and greatly increase the rate at which an appropriate and successful solution is developed.

Experienced professionals are usually highly detail-oriented about their profession or skill because they've seen so many scenarios before, tried various solutions, have seen and made numerous mistakes themselves, and have seen the results of all of them.

What Is The Right Amount of Knowledge?

It depends (but you knew that already). In work environments, education and training tend to be provided as need arises, erring on the side of too little, especially for those with too few resources or simply a relaxed culture regarding employee development. Companies that invest in employee education and training generally experience a strong return on the investment.

The appropriate amount of knowledge required for any task, role, or position depends upon the minimum required competency or standard of quality that has been set for the task. The requirement (or lack thereof) may be defined by an individual, industry standards, society, regulatory agencies, the company handbook, the organization's quality standards, or any other set of rules or norms. As mentioned before, critical tasks, functions, or roles in society tend to be highly regulated and/or controlled in order to sustain a minimal level of risk, safety, and value for society. That is, when people tend to get injured or killed while doing something, someone tends to make rules around it.

Some tasks or jobs require little-to-no specialized education to be performed at an adequate level, but education and/or training requirements will increase along with competency requirements or other quality or duty of care standards. There are jobs people are often willing to fill with someone who has no prior experience or training (or even "anyone with a pulse"). Brief instruction and minimal on the job training is sufficient to get the job done initially. Starting positions in manual labor (unskilled), light-reception, and janitorial are examples of jobs in which prior experience is often not required for new hires. If greater opportunity or value is realized in the position or person, additional education or training may be provided and/or even required for future hires.

On the other hand, because a higher degree of competency is expected, some professions require specialized education and/or training/apprenticeship -- or even licensure -- before an individual is allowed to perform them professionally without oversight. Plumbers, electricians, and many other trade professionals fall into this category.

The knowledge standards of some professions are self-regulated within their industries through certifications, association memberships, or other similar non-governmental requirements. For example, some companies looking to hire a quality control professional may only hire someone with a Six Sigma certification to ensure a minimal level of education. IT industry professionals are familiar with Microsoft, Cisco, and other well-known credentials used for selecting new hires.

Finally, there are professions such as doctors and some engineers in which success or failure of an individual task or project is potentially so critical or valuable that years of education *and* extensive training or apprenticeship are required before a person can begin working independently, take responsibility for, or "sign off on," his or her own work.

The Main Point about Knowledge

As it relates to attention to detail, knowledge needs to be considered for two primary reasons:

- **When a mistake or error has been made and recognized**, consideration should be given to whether or not the individual who made the mistake has received or accumulated the proper amount of education, training, or experience. This is often overlooked, and the person is simply told to "pay more attention to detail" with little or no additional feedback or instruction provided.
- **When you are creating a system** for a specific task or process you should consider how much education or training is required for each step and design the processes and procedures around that, as well as according to who will be performing the task or procedure. Make sure it accounts for future employees as well as existing.

Knowledge -- education, training, and experience -- should always be considered when attempting to improve or address an individual or group's attention to detail.

Interest

De gustibus non disputandum est.
Latin saying: About taste, you cannot argue.

Your level of interest for any particular task or topic may range from complete apathy about *any* possible outcome to an intense passion about the *right* outcome. That is, for a given task or role it is possible that you may absolutely *not care less* about total failure while, for another task or role, you would fight to the death to ensure a specific outcome. Fortunately, the great majority of tasks don't require a fight to the death for success.

Interest vs. Motivation

You may be thinking this sounds an awful lot like motivation. And, you can make an argument that we could be talking about motivation here, but I don't like the word motivation in this context. I don't feel it appropriately describes the spirit of interest in the context of attention to detail. As a term, we tend to use motivation in a sort of negative tone. Motivation is often used as a word for manipulating someone's behavior into a specific action. Interest, on the other hand, is somewhat more wholesome. It is more genuine. To become more detail-oriented in a matter, to improve your attention to detail, you need to develop interest. Motivation may drive some kind of short-term behavior, and that can be positive. In fact, you may need some sort of motivation to initiate developing your interest in your topic or task. Unlike motivation, true interest is what makes you curious and makes you want to regularly improve. Interest is intrinsic.

Several factors contribute to your level of interest in a task. These are the factors I consider most important:

- Obligation
- Enjoyment
- Relevance
- Criticality
- Rewards

If you are struggling with a position or specific task, consider addressing each of these as they relate to the task. You may be surprised as to what you find. Simply by labeling or applying a value to each you may find that you can approach the task with a more open and fresh perspective.

Obligation

An obligation to perform a task to some specified level is a common motivator (perhaps the most common) for attention to detail. Legally-speaking, there are two types of obligations -- perfect and imperfect. Perfect obligations involve the legal requirement of an action (or inaction) or delivery. Imperfect obligations are essentially moral obligations; they do not place a legal requirement of performance or delivery upon anyone.

In terms of everyday situations, I submit that there are three types of obligation, broadly speaking -- personal, professional, and legal.

Personal (or Moral) Obligations

We regularly take on personal obligations whose performance requires little more than simple contrastive attention to detail. For example, you might tell your son or daughter, "I'll take you to the zoo this weekend." You either will or will not go to the zoo this weekend (contrastive). If you care about building trust and rapport with your child, you will at least drop by the zoo at some point during the weekend for a quick walk around. Alternatively, you may promise to your son or daughter, "Your birthday party will be the best party anyone at your school has ever seen." Assuming you are doing the party planning yourself, this statement implies a certain level of performance that will at least require analytical attention to detail as well as a splash of additive attention to detail. You may also need a pony.

Professional Obligations

Businesses commonly place subtle, non-legal obligations upon themselves and their employees to perform to a certain level. For example, if a department store manager or owner decides to advertise "Unparalleled Customer Service" but fails to adequately inform and/or train the staff for this new level of expectation, there may be a disconnect between what the customer expects and what is experienced in the store. If a sales associate is rude or even generally less than great, that obligation of "unparalleled customer service" has not been met and the customer will be disappointed, at the very least. There is no legal repercussion for this failure but, in the world of online reviews and traditional word of mouth marketing, it could certainly have negative impacts on the store's reputation and sales.

An owner or manager who is particularly aware of this obligation will ensure that the proper level of communication, training, and other systems are in place to assure employees behavior is in line with the advertised promises and obligations.

Legal Obligations

Obligation is commonly a legal matter. Legal obligations apply to everyday business transactions, large and complex contractual agreements, and even many personal situations. Legal obligations are driven by the requirement to meet specific conditions or to perform, or not perform, certain actions based on defined, or even just reasonable, expectations.

First, it should be clear that this is not a legal book, I am in no way an expert on legal matters, and you should not refer to this book or its contents for information related to the proper handling of any legal matter whatsoever. To illustrate the complexity and importance of attention to detail I am including a list of the types of legal obligation. Though they are sometimes grouped differently, depending on the source, these are the types of legal obligation:

1. Pure obligations
2. Conditional obligations
3. Obligations with a period
4. Alternative obligations
5. Joint obligations
6. Solidary obligations
7. Divisible obligation
8. Indivisible obligation
9. Obligation with a penal clause

In each of these cases, there is a legal expectation of delivery or performance. If that expectation is not met, the offending party can be held liable and responsible for payment in some way.

Legal obligation is a huge driver of interest in attention to detail for the obvious reason of minimizing liability. You want to make sure to "get it right" so you don't have to pay a penalty.

You can plainly see there is overlap between legal, professional, and personal obligations. For instance, while you are contractually and legally obligated to deliver X number of units to your customer on or before the delivery date, your primary motivation for doing so is probably professional because you want to uphold your reputation and earn repeat business. Even though you may be doing everything you can because you want a great review on Google, your customer could be thinking, "If they don't perform, I have legal options."

Enjoyment

Someone said, and then multitudes of people afterward repeated, "Love what you do and you'll never work a day in your life." While I'm not convinced it's true all the time, it gets to the point of the relationship between enjoyment and attention to detail.

Hobbies demonstrate the most obvious example of high attention to detail driven by interest. People spend hundreds -- even thousands -- of dollars on their hobbies and perform them with excellence purely out of enjoyment. The concept applies whether the hobby is making something, such as model building, or is some kind of sport, such as kayaking. A dedicated model builder may spend a small (or large) fortune on materials such as kits, paints, tools, and more, and then spend dozens or hundreds of hours creating an impeccable, perfectly-scaled model. Likewise, a kayaker will spend thousands of dollars on kayaks, gear, and equipment, and then hundreds or thousands of hours on the water -- sometimes in life-threatening conditions. In both scenarios, the drive to spend the money and do what they do is based on interest and enjoyment. There's usually no prize money, no extrinsic reward other than, perhaps, being part of the associated community of other like-minded hobbyists.

In a work environment, enjoyment of the task at hand is seldom the main driver of interest. I can hear my mom saying, "That's why it's called work." and there's some truth to that. Most people are not lucky enough to work at something they might otherwise do for free. And, even for those who are lucky enough, there are always tasks -- ranging from mundane daily tasks to complex problems -- that simply have to be dealt with. Even the professional, sponsored kayaker still has to do some bookkeeping, read the occasional contract, and work on business development. Salespeople who love sales (and there are many of them) are somewhat notorious for hating the backend details involved in the nurturing and closing of a sale -- reporting, updating CRM, forecasting, following up with customers, and so on.

Some tasks are simply no fun. Unless you can make a specific task more fun (i.e. by making a game of it, keeping a score of some kind, competing with a coworker, etc.), you may simply have to get through it the best you can.

Criticality

There are certain situations in which strong attention to detail is driven largely by the *importance* of proper performance of the task.

This can be similar to obligation in some cases, but there are distinct differences. You may have an obligation to perform something correctly without it being critical. Criticality is relevant for situations of safety or situations in which failure may have a catastrophic outcome. That outcome could be anything from total failure of the project to loss of money, loss of reputation, or even loss of life. For instance, engineers who design airplanes understand the importance of the quality of their work, so extreme attention to detail is built into aircraft design through complex systems involving numerous checklists, reviews at various levels, testing and retesting, more reviews, and numerous test flights.

The major requirement in order for criticality to play a role in increasing attention to detail is *awareness* of the critical nature of the task. If the forklift driver is unaware of the fragile nature of the cargo he is picking up, then criticality will not play a role in increasing his interest in doing it right.

Relevance

In the context of work, employees like to know that what they are doing is meaningful. What kind of quality would you expect is put into a task when the person performing it is thinking, "It doesn't matter anyway" or is wondering why they are even doing it? Unfortunately, many people perform tasks whose full meaning and importance they do not understand. For them, they are just completing a form, preparing a document, counting inventory, or scheduling a delivery because they were told to and, for whatever reason, their role in the process feels irrelevant or unimportant to them. They do not understand or appreciate the impact their individual performance -- good or bad -- can have on the next person in the process, the end-user, the customer, and maybe even on themselves.

That someone understands the purpose of a given task is an easy assumption for a manager or co-worker to make. Likewise, it is a relatively easy thing to remedy -- both in the moment and systemically. A simple conversation may be enough for some circumstances, but, ideally, consideration should be given to the initial training process and to ongoing conversations about the importance of a person's role in the organization and how his or her work impacts others. Ideally, understanding the value of individual employees and the roles they play is a feature of the company's culture.

Here is an exercise you may find helpful for yourself or others if you feel unclear about your role or suspect a coworker or employee does not understand his role(s) in a process. Ask him to draw a simple flow chart or write down the steps of the process including where his actions lie. You both may find the exercise enlightening and may even see opportunities for improvement in the process. This is also a fantastic team exercise and you do not need to wait until there's a problem to bring it to your team.

Rewards

It is important to keep context in mind for this section. Rewards generally drive extrinsic motivation as opposed to a sincere *interest* in a concern or goal. *In the context of increasing interest in order to improve attention to detail,* rewards do not generally address the central problems that may be leading to errors, mistakes, or less-than-optimal outcomes.

For some tasks, there may be rewards sufficient to create interest *in performing the task well enough to get the reward,* but it is generally not a good long-term solution for ongoing issues with attention to detail. For lasting results, you will probably always need to go a step further.

Self-rewards: An individual may try attaching a reward to the correct completion of a task or goal. For instance, after you complete your "TPS" reports, perhaps you deserve a walking break or even a cookie. This may work nicely for an individual but is likely to have limited success at the organizational level.

Using a reward to uncover a solution: A manager or team lead may find that higher levels of productivity occur when rewards are offered to employees to reach a short-term improvement objective or productivity boost. The successful achievement of the goal and reward(s) could lead to a thorough analysis of *how* the improvements were achieved and *that could* lead to a system that creates sustainable improvements. Something to consider: If the team does not achieve the goal and does not get the reward, it is possible they will be less motivated to try other reward-based improvements.

Before trying rewards to correct an attention to detail issue, first consider the other elements of interest as well as the other 4 fundamental elements -- Knowledge, Systems, Focus, and Attitude.

Systems

We use systems to streamline, automate, or perform certain functions or tasks to deliver more accurate and/or consistent outcomes. We do it without thinking about it. How often do you pick up a calculator to double-check your math or to simply let it do that math for you? You probably don't think about your attention to detail when you do math (and you don't usually need to) but you are aware there is only one answer and that you will either get it right or wrong.

If you plan to perform a task more than a few times and accuracy is important, consider developing a system that will move the attentional requirement from your head onto paper or into an electronic format such as a spreadsheet, computer, or app. This is especially true for complex or multi-step processes.

Here is a list of systems you may consider using:

- Repetition
- Reminders
- Checklists
- Review, feedback, and verification
- Calculators and logical tools
- Rules & guidelines
- Standardization
- Charts & graphs
- Manuals

Let's expand upon them a little. Entire books are available for several of these systems; we are only going to touch upon them lightly, primarily for the purpose of idea generation. There are countless applications for the various systems and your specific challenge(s) may be solved by one system or by the combination of two or more. You will recognize the fact that systems quickly meld and, at some point, you may need to switch from one to another. You will have to decide for yourself at which points your routine becomes a checklist (or vice versa) or when your checklist becomes a more complex process or set of rules and where they all fit into your manuals.

Routine or Repetition

If you never want to lose your keys again, always put them in the same place. Always. Routine is one of the simplest and most basic of systems, and only requires a small amount of dedication.

Your routine could simply be that you always put something back in the same place or it could be that you always perform a specific action at the beginning of any task. Routines are common for simple safety-related concerns. For instance, before driving away, a semi-truck driver may do a walk-around of his truck and loaded trailer to inspect and confirm that all straps are tightened securely, that there are no loose boards on the trailer, that all hoses and lines are connected properly, that all tires are ok (visibly), and that there are no problems in general.

A checklist could be used in place of a routine in some cases, but there are instances where a checklist may be too complex for the concern at hand (lost keys) or the flexibility of a routine may prove more thorough than a checklist (the many variations of a loaded truck).

Reminders

This one is almost an eye roller but it is also a reality and the cause of frustration. The most common reason for the "I forgot" excuse is that people don't create a reminder. They either think they will remember on their own or they get distracted in the moment they were going to create the reminder.

We all use reminders regularly. Reminders can be as low-tech as a sticky note, a date on your calendar or in your planner, or your grandmother's suggestion of tying a string around your finger. Alternatively, there are numerous technology solutions for reminders such as timers, alarms, scheduling systems, and so on. Do whatever works best for you or your organization.

Checklists

I love checklists and use them every day. A properly developed checklist -- even a simple one in many cases -- can take the productivity and performance of an individual, a team, or an entire organization to the next level.

Checklists can be broad to cover an organization's primary quarterly or yearly objectives (with underlying metrics, of course) or specifically created for a single, detailed task.

A properly developed and executed checklist is the most cost-effective system an individual or organization can quickly put into place to reduce errors, ensure thoroughness, and increase overall productivity. In day to day life, they can keep a person's day moving along smoothly and ensure everything gets done. For specific tasks, they help ensure nothing is forgotten or overlooked. Checklists are used extensively in the medical industry to literally save lives by preventing countless surgical and other medical mishaps.[25] A well-made checklist can enable an inexperienced person to complete a task or project with the thoroughness and accuracy of an experienced professional. Just as important, a checklist may simply enable a tired or overwhelmed individual to complete a task correctly and thoroughly.

A note of caution: Checklists have an inherent potential weakness. In cases where circumstances fall outside normal operations, the specified checklist may not be adequate. The individual(s) or team executing the actions required by the checklist must be able to deviate and act accordingly.

A checklist may not be your *final* solution to a challenge or issue, but it may be the fastest and most cost-effective way to make a real and lasting impact during the process of finding the ultimate solution.

Review and Verification

By default, this goes beyond an *individual's* attention to detail. At least one additional person is being

---

[25] Gawande, Atul. *The Checklist Manifesto: How to Get Things Right.* Metropolitan Books, New York, 2010

brought into the mix, making this an organizational concern. The requirement for a review or verification is generally set by a rule within the organization, or by a regulation of some type.

Usually the work being reviewed was initially completed by a less experienced individual or team, but this is not always the case. Depending upon value and criticality, many complex projects or issues require a second (and maybe a third or fourth) pair of eyes and/or higher level of experience to consider the accuracy, options, legal concerns, or potential repercussions of a given proposal or solution.

Many trades and professions require, by governmental regulation, terms of apprenticeship or internship during which the trainee's work is overseen and approved by a senior professional.

Senior legal counsel will almost certainly review the work of junior attorneys or paralegals before presenting documents or heading to court. Sales teams commonly have a rule that any proposal over a certain dollar amount must be reviewed by a manager before being presented to the client. Some industries, such as aerospace, require numerous layers of review before even a single component of an airplane can be approved for use. Quality control departments are created specifically for the purpose of review and/or verification.

Tools for Calculation & Cognitive Efficiency

One definition of "tool" is "Something used in performing an operation or necessary in the practice of a vocation or profession."[26] Countless tools are available to help you improve your attention to detail, decrease errors, work more efficiently, and more effectively overall. Instead of going into details about the various types of tools here I am simply providing a list of examples of tools. After some thought and research, you will probably find there is *some* version

---

[26] Merriam-Webster Dictionary. *Search: "tool"*. merriam-webster.com. Accessed 9/3/2018.

(likely many versions) of the tools designed especially for your industry, profession, or even for your specific task at hand.

In the context of being more detail-oriented, the purposes of the tools are to help you use your cognitive resources more efficiently and effectively, reduce the need for knowledge, reduce or eliminate human error, and/or to enable a higher level of thoroughness. Here is a list of tools you may be able to use:

- Checklists and/or reminders
- Spreadsheets
- Maps & calendars
- Software
- Calculator(s)
- Charts & graphs
- Reference materials & books
- Timers, alarms, time-trackers
- Rulers, micrometers, compasses, protractors
- Apps, extensions, plugins, etc.
- Wheel charts & slide charts
- Optical Mark Resolution (OMR; aka, "Scantron")
- Templates
- "Cheat Sheets"

This list is not meant to be comprehensive or all-inclusive. Rather, I hope it spurs an idea for a tool or set of tools you have at hand or could procure or create to help you with some task or challenge.

Having tools at hand means you can quickly identify and/or process the relevant elements to bring about a more accurate or appropriate solution. Furthermore, the right tools will do much of the "thinking" for you so you can focus more mindfully on the task.

Rules & Guidelines

While processes and procedures -- to be covered in the next section -- tell you what to do and *how to do it*, rules and guidelines provide strategic direction and parameters within which you should focus your efforts. Rules and guidelines generally allow for flexibility and creativity in the process of producing desired outcomes or deliverables. They are the minimum and maximum (even if only budgetary) requirements or limits; the specifications for what must be developed and/or delivered.

Clarity of expectations is important for the effective use and execution of rules and guidelines. The creator of them needs to use a reasonable level of specificity as well as language common to the person or persons who will be performing the task, completing the project, or otherwise expected to abide by them. The specifications for a bridge cannot simply say, "Facilitate transportation to the other side and make it big and grand." That may make an architect's mouth water, but it is likely to end with some intended requirements unfulfilled and/or gross overspending. The bridge may not be high enough to allow for occasional boat traffic or it may not be strong enough to accommodate heavy commercial traffic and so on. The example is extreme, but it gets the point across. The rules and guidelines -- the specifications -- for the construction of a bridge need to include details about traffic volume requirements, expected commercial traffic, boat traffic (if any), and budget at an absolute bare minimum. The specifications combined with other information such as climate, water levels, soil types, span, and more can then be combined to develop any number of design possibilities that meet the detailed specifications.

Rules and guidelines can be used to affect workplace behavior, as well. From the overarching strategic direction of the company or team to compliance issues to expected workplace dress and behavior, rules and guidelines are used to set the focus and boundaries that act as direction and governance for employees and other constituents. Within the defined boundaries is a sort of free space where anything is possible, to an extent.

Processes, Procedures, & Manuals

Documented processes and procedures define and describe the appropriate series of actions or steps that need to happen in order to achieve a specific outcome. They facilitate proficiency and consistency for individuals and organizations and reduce or remove the need for knowledge by guiding decisions and providing instruction. They even contribute to an individual's efficient use of cognitive resources by allowing the person to focus on the task in the moment instead of planning steps, deciding what to do now, and thinking about what comes next.

If you are performing a task that will be completed multiple times, invest time in writing a process and/or procedure(s) for it. This is especially true if *someone else* will be performing the task. Think of all the processes completed every day at your office. How much time was spent training people to do those tasks? How many times did they get it wrong after their initial "training"? Written processes and procedures greatly reduce the amount of time required for training people as well as the number of mistakes made when they take on the tasks independently. You can save yourself and others countless hours of time learning and/or re-learning how to do things, where to find answers, what needs to be done next, and so on. The net result is a sizeable increase in productivity and reduction in cost (and stress).

What is the difference between processes and procedures? The two terms get confusing and are often used interchangeably. Here's how I like to simplify the difference: Think of a process as a flow chart (a system) comprised of various procedures (task sequences) that must be completed in order to achieve the goal or desired outcome of the process. The procedure may be as simple as making a decision based on certain criteria, or it could be a multi-step task completed via a machine or computer.

Manuals: Putting It All In One Place

A manual is a set or collection of instructions -- including procedures, policies, guidelines, and more -- for a related purpose. Some manuals are specific to a single task, function, operation, or service. Others, such as "company manuals" or "standard operating procedures" may be broader in scope and outline the processes, procedures, policies, and guidelines of entire departments or organizations.

Manuals are excellent training and reference resources to prepare and empower employees with the information and guidance they need to understand complete systems and perform tasks and functions accurately and efficiently.

Examples of manuals include:

- Employee manual (often called "handbook")
- Service manual
- Product manual
- Operations manual
- Standard Operating Procedures (SOP) manual
- Sales manual
- Maintenance manual
- Systems Manual
- And anything else that needs a documented collection of processes and policies in one place

Few businesses use manuals as effectively as they could, especially small businesses. According to a survey by HR services company, Gusto, only 26 percent of small businesses have an employee handbook[27] which matches estimates I have heard anecdotally from various sources. Many businesses that do have employee handbooks do not effectively deploy them for use and reference by employees. Additionally, handbooks are not updated often enough to remain relevant. In this day and age, significant consideration should be given to the optimal platform for a company's handbook. If what you do and/or how it is done changes quickly, perhaps printed manuals are not needed. A virtual version which can be kept up to date in real time may be ideal while saving huge amounts of paper and money.

The larger an organization becomes, the more specialized its manuals will become. A tiny organization of five people can probably use a single "Operations Manual" that details nearly *everything* the company does including sales, marketing, hiring and employee policies, payroll, financing and accounting practices, to production and services. As the company grows, those business functions will each need their own manuals in order to keep them reasonably current, relevant, and generally manageable. Individual

---

[27] Gusto. Infographic. "Employee Handbooks: The good, the bad, and the awesome." https://gusto.com/framework/hr/small-businesses-employee-handbooks-stand-infographic/, accessed 9/17/2018.

organizations and teams need role-specific manuals to facilitate fast employee onboarding and training for new systems, software, and methods. Regardless of the size of an organization, a manual -- and the policies, procedures, processes, checklists, and information it includes -- can help make individuals and the overall organization more efficient, effective, productive, and profitable.

Right or Wrong Attitude (RoW)

Those involved in a task must have clarity about what is right and what is not. Everyone needs to be dedicated to understanding that "It's either right or wrong" and then to "Getting it right" every time. Unfortunately, as previously discussed, haste, negligence, laziness, tiredness, lack of focus, apathy, and a handful of other factors often impair the dedication to getting it right, and it gets left at "good enough" (and it usually isn't).

For contrastive attention to detail, "Right" and "Wrong" are pre-defined because there is only one solution. The feedback is typically immediate and can be verified or checked. The light is on or off, the box is checked or not, the math is correct or not, the numbers match or they do not, the trash has been taken out or not. It is either done or not; It's right or its wrong.

Analytical attention to detail may have multiple correct or appropriate solutions and they may not be so obvious. Verification by other people or systems may be needed to ensure accomplishment and, even then, there may be some amount of subjectivity. Whether you and your team has developed and implemented the most effective strategy for company growth – as compared to all other possibilities – remains to be determined until the strategy has been in place for some time. And, even after it proves to be successful, there may still be arguments that other possible solutions would have been even more successful. **Probably the most important component of analytical attention to detail is thoroughness.** You need to ensure that all the elements of the issue/challenge/task have been addressed to the best of your abilities and resources -- within reason, in consideration of the importance, value, and criticality of the task. I fully understand how obvious that might sound to you. The fact is that most people simply do not apply the appropriate level of thoroughness to the tasks they take on. They do not consider and/or address all the important elements, factors, possibilities, options, solutions, outcomes, and contingencies for a given concern before deciding upon a solution. Thoroughness, or lack of it, always eventually becomes apparent.

For matters related to additive attention to detail -- where the goal is improvement or innovation of some kind -- what is regarded as "Right" or "Wrong" is subjective, or user-defined, because the desired outcome is specified, or defined by the creator(s) or innovator(s). Regardless of this subjectivity, the specification(s) for what is right and/or wrong should be clear to those who need to create the end result. Without this clarity, the end result will be impossible to achieve without multiple iterations and re-do's. As with analytical attention to detail, thoroughness is again perhaps the key. Absolute thoroughness.

A Dedication to Last Touch Delivery

It is interesting to me how a dedication to getting things right seems to be ingrained in some people. Maybe it's because of specific influences in their upbringing ("Grandpa always said...") or perhaps they just see things in black and white. Or, for specific tasks, they may simply have an exceptionally high level of interest in creating a specific outcome. It could be those and one-hundred other things, as well.

In the work environment, I often refer to this as a dedication to "last touch delivery" because at the end of the day, that is what it's really about. An employee with a high level of attention to detail combined with a dedication to getting it right is much more likely to turn in work that is ready for delivery -- ready for the customer, for presenting to upper management, for the next step of the process; it is complete. The employee's manager can review it but won't have to touch it due to errors or omissions. Because of that employee's last touch delivery, the manager (and coworkers) don't have to spend time editing and/or correcting the work and can spend her time on more important things. This makes the employee more valuable overall while saving time and money on labor and re-do's and protecting the manager's, team's, and/or company's reputation for producing quality work.

Clarifying what is Right or Wrong enables employees to develop a dedication to last touch delivery because they understand what the end result should look like.

Employees generally want to do a good job, but many are not quite motivated enough to do the work of *finding out what a "good job" is*. We've all said, "I wasn't really sure what you wanted but..." RoW clarity removes that barrier so the employee can work on the project with confidence about the right outcome. This is especially true for Analytical and Additive attention to detail. Contrastive attention to detail is essentially self-defined. It's either right or wrong.

Developing a Detail-Oriented Organization

This book focuses primarily on developing and improving individuals' attention to detail in the context of work and working environments. How can we apply it to the organization as a whole?

What if everyone in the organization performed just a little better? What if each person made one, two, or three mistakes – even tiny ones -- every day? Even better, what if everyone is simply able to focus more effectively? This could not only mean work is completed more quickly but also that deliverables are of higher quality. If people are more focused, they are likely to generate better ideas and produce better solutions and innovations. I could go on. When people get things right or simply perform better across the board, the organization benefits. Creating a detail-oriented organization starts with individuals who are detail-oriented and respect and value it in the people around them.

The full discussion of developing a more detail-oriented organization is beyond the scope of this book but there are some core concepts I want to leave for any manager or leader interested in affecting change in his or her organization. A culture of attention to detail can be created by emphasizing the importance of getting the little things right every day and identifying and addressing problems and opportunities for improvement. Details of the customer experience, product quality and usability, how people are treated, how clean the break room is, whether the paint on the sign in front is faded or not, if various benefits are valued by employees, office communications, and much more should be addressed. The opportunities for improvements are everywhere.

Here are some core concepts that are important for developing a detail-oriented culture.

Make it a Visible Company Value: It is important that the importance of attention to detail is visible to everyone. Some places where it can be made visible are through training, visual reminders such as posters, in the language used by leadership, and in shared stories and examples of successes.

Help Everyone Understand Roles & Impact: People who are unsure of how, or if, what they do matters in an organization or even to those around them are likely to be less interested in the quality or outcome of their work. Use organizational and team charts, process flow charts, meetings, straightforward discussions, and even simple appreciation to ensure people understand how and why what they do matters.

Train and Develop: If people are to get things right, you should ensure they've been taught the proper way(s) to do those things. Invest in training people. Additionally, make job-specific education and training the first topic when someone appears to be struggling with performance.

Minimize Distractions: Allow and even empower people to minimize needless distractions and create an atmosphere where people respect and appreciate the concept of focus and being able to work with minimal interruptions. This is easier for some roles than others but should be possible to some degree in almost any position, especially in office settings.

Clarify What Success Looks Like: At all levels, communications should help people understand what they are trying to achieve. From the primary company mission down to the team and task levels, people should have enough clarity to be able to make decisions about which actions and outcomes are right and which would be wrong.

Develop Systems: Develop or procure systems and enable people to create systems that help improve consistency, increase accuracy, remove human error, and generally automate attention to detail. You might consider an audit of your existing systems to (a) discover what you may already have but have forgotten, (b) make updates or improvements, and (c) raise awareness about useful systems that already exist.

Developing a culture of attention to detail will take some time but your people will make it happen if given the proper training, information, empowerment, and respect to do so.

Pay Attention to "The Big Picture" Too

After all this focus on the details, I feel compelled to remind you of the importance of "The Big Picture." People sometimes ask me about this after a workshop or via email. They usually ask something like, "Can you be both a big picture thinker *and* detail-oriented?" or they'll just say, "yeah, but what about the bigger picture?"

Here's the thing: They are not mutually-exclusive. At all. They are both important. "The big picture" is where you position your goals, your purpose, and your dreams. The big picture is all about the where and they why – where you are going and why you are going there.

The details make progress happen. They're the steps you take. Your attention to the details largely determines your level of success in reaching your goals, in fulfilling your purpose, and living your dreams. The details are the how, the what, the who, then when. These concepts are the same at the individual and organizational levels.

Do some people tend to put more energy into one or the other? Yes, most do. Is it possible to attend to both? Absolutely! And, it is important – critical even – that you do so. It's not hard. Maybe you need to write your goals down, put reminders up, make posters, whatever it takes.

Ask the most successful people you know about the importance of the big picture and the details. The majority of them are probably primarily focused on the big picture, but nearly all will agree that the details are essential. Those that prefer not to deal with the details themselves (many love them) typically automate them in some way. They have systems in place and/or people to take care of them. I've even met an interesting business owner who preferred to spend his time focusing on "the details." He owns a software company and prefers the technical aspects of programming and developing solutions at the ground level. While this technician-owner arrangement stifles numerous small businesses, his company is doing great because he understands the importance of "the big picture" enough that he hired someone else to be the President of his company – to take care of the big picture.

So, I'll leave it at that. The big picture and the details are both important, and you can manage them both. In fact, if you discover that you are not clear about *your* big picture, go ahead and add that to your checklist. It could be the most important detail to take care of before moving on to the others.

Thank you! Want to Connect?

I hope you enjoyed this book and got a lot out of it.

If you would like to learn more, have additional questions or comments, or if you are interested in working with me please go to www.AttentionToDetail.com.

Attention To Detail Training & Consulting

I offer additional Attention To Detail Training as well as consulting.

Online Courses: Great for individuals who want to learn to develop well-rounded attention via online video courses. To thank you for purchasing the book, use the code ATD20 when you checkout to receive a 20% discount on your purchase.

Live Workshops: I offer employee training and development workshops. The main course is a 3.5-hour workshop including active and engaging individual and group exercises. Available everywhere airplanes, cars, trains, and boats go.

Consulting: I am available for consulting to develop and/or improve attention to detail in your team(s) or entire organization. Whether you want to make some cultural adjustments to be more detail-oriented or meet specific performance goals, I can help. Call me at 832-301-6075 or contact me via AttentionToDetail.com.

Made in the USA
Middletown, DE
10 November 2021